Forty Ways to Say I Love You

*For Christian couples who want
to keep their love alive*

Forty Ways to Say I Love You

James R. Bjorge

AUGSBURG Publishing House • Minneapolis

FORTY WAYS TO SAY I LOVE YOU

Copyright © 1978 Augsburg Publishing House

Library of Congress Catalog Card No. 78-52179

International Standard Book No. 0-8066-1654-7

Scripture quotations unless otherwise noted are from the Revised Standard Version of the Bible, copyright 1946, 1952, and 1971 by the Division of Christian Education of the National Council of Churches.

MANUFACTURED IN THE UNITED STATES OF AMERICA

To my wife, Fran

Contents

page 9   Preface

      11   I will cooperate

      13   I will say it today

      15   I will pause to ponder

      17   I will use my imagination

      19   I will help you grow

      21   I will be a team player

      23   I will refuel romance

      25   I will give you freedom

      27   I will let you be you

      29   I will look for the best

      31   I will laugh with you, not at you

      33   I will practice the proper touch

      35   I will keep myself for you

      37   I will prime the pump

      39   I will answer softly

      41   I will label my actions

      43   I will care for others

      45   I will love you with my mind

      47   I will love our relatives

      49   I will look for newness

      51   I will hear your viewpoint

53　I will pause to wonder

55　I will keep singing

57　I will strive for the best

59　I will give it my all

61　I will be gentle

63　I will face the future

65　I will keep love hot

67　I will give myself away

69　I will try to understand

71　I will love you even if you fail

73　I will keep saying it

75　I will tell you when I'm upset

77　I will use God's blueprint

79　I will make our house a home

81　I will be standing by

83　I will take inventory

85　I will seal you with the cross

87　I will pray for us

89　I will keep climbing

91　Prayer for partners

93　The way of love

Preface

A music box plays one tune over and over again. It is simply a mechanical operation. But a marriage is a living relationship that cannot be boxed in with the melody of a single tune. Love is dynamic, growing, constantly creating new songs of spirit and substance.

A telephone answering service repeats the same message continuously when the number is dialed. Its operation is programmed and sterile. Two people in love cannot afford to respond with pat, predictable comments. Love develops an openness and freshness which enables conversation to communicate sensitivity and concern.

Forty Ways to Say I Love You is designed to unlock creative potential in Christian couples who are endeavoring to keep their love alive through exciting ways of saying "I love you" by word and deed.

1

I will cooperate

God liked pairs, so he made a pair of persons. He called them man and woman. They were the same, yet they were different. When old Noah gathered his family and the menagerie into the huge wooden ark, they came filing in, two by two.

I was given two arms. They are the same, yet my right hand is stronger. It does the writing. It throws the ball. It has certain abilities developed through years of use. However, it never lords it over the left arm. Right and left work beautifully together as I catch a ball, eat a meal, or hug my wife. They are companions, not competitors.

I have two eyes, yet I see one image. I have never examined my eyes to discover if one is stronger than the other. Neither one argues about having to do more than its share in the workload of seeing. Neither one strives to view more than the other. They exist to fortify each other.

I have two legs. I can kick a ball farther with

my right foot than with my left, but I could not walk or run unless both willingly transported my body. They cooperate and complement each other, making me mobile.

These pairs of organs and appendages comprising the person that is me could develop problems if they weren't centrally controlled. All parts of the body accept the position of the head, which governs the whole.

God made persons with the possibility of being pairs. "Therefore a man leaves his father and his mother and cleaves to his wife, and they become one flesh" (Gen. 2:24). Pairs of persons are to function as one, as do pairs of eyes, hands, and feet. Together a woman and man can do more than either can do individually.

But here is the rub. Who controls the working of this marital body? Maybe the only answer is that we allow Christ to be the head of the house as he is the head of the church. Easy? No. But in the spirit of his love we can work at love together for the good of the whole. Then it is not a question of who is right, but what is right.

Love is working together.

2

I will say it today

Ole and Olga lived on a farm in Iowa. Olga was living on a starvation diet of affection. Ole never gave her any signs of love, and Olga's need to be appreciated went unfulfilled. At her wit's end, Olga blurted out, "Ole, why don't you ever tell me that you love me?" Ole stoically responded, "Olga, when we were married I told you that I loved you, and if I ever change my mind I'll let you know."

That is not enough. Remember in the Old Testament the account of the Israelites wandering in the Sinai desert? During those arduous days God provided them with manna for their physical sustenance. It came fresh each morning like dew on the grass. Some Israelites wanted security for their tomorrows, so they tried to gather a supply for several days at one time. It always spoiled and became full of worms. God seemed to be telling them that he would daily supply their needs. He wanted them to daily be aware of their dependence on his goodness.

Other things besides manna cannot be stored, pickled, or embalmed. One is love. Love cannot be stored in a trunk for a rainy day. It cannot be guaranteed by signing a document of intent. It lives each day—only when fresh.

My wife bakes buns and sweet rolls each week. Some are frozen for the days ahead. When thawed they are good, but in no way do they measure up to their delicious freshness on the morning they're popped out of the oven. Then the kitchen has an aroma of old-style baking, and the rolls are warm and soft and melt in the mouth. You can't beat freshness.

In marriage, many good things may have happened in the yesterdays. You may have sung love songs, whispered affection, and passionately embraced. But if not baked fresh today, affection soon becomes stale, and we find ourselves famished for the fresh food of love.

So say it today. Do it today. Feast on the newness of your love.

Love is new each day.

3

I will pause to ponder

We are a people on the run. We worship quickness. Grocery stores feature minute rice, minute tapioca, and minute steaks. We gulp down our instant coffee and instant tea. When we set out on a trip, arrival at the destination looms large, and we forget to look at the landscape along the way. Sociologists tell us we even make love too fast.

We race through childhood robbing those few precious years of their joys. Soft, cuddly Raggedy Ann dolls used to make pillows for tired little heads. Now they've been replaced by fashion-model dolls with figures that bulge in all the right places. Little girls, eager to grow up quickly and look like the dolls, breathlessly await their first bras.

As a boy I'd wander through the orchard, impatient for the apples to ripen. Sometimes in a moment of impatience I'd devour a few green ones. They were sour and the end result was a stomachache. I learned the virtue of patience the hard way.

But when we arrive at marriage and have said our respective "I do's," then, as never before, patience is a prerequisite for harmony.

We want a house and a new car before we can afford them. We want security without struggle. We want complete compatibility before we've worked out adjustments. We want automatic peaks of sexual fulfillment before we've learned what the two of us enjoy.

Slow down. You will destroy the miracle of life by rushing it. Inch by inch makes companionship a cinch. Be patient with each other, for God is working in both of you when you let him.

And remember—dreams are worth waiting for.

Love is willing to wait.

4

I will use my imagination

A friend of mine is an alcoholic who was touched by the hand of the Healing Physician and delivered from the bondage of the bottle. An extremely talented man, he began to direct all his energies to serving the liberating Lord. Along the way he met a young woman who caught his eye and captured his heart. A lengthy courtship was consummated in wedding bells.

He had their classy honeymoon suite decorated with roses and gaily lit candles that gave a dancing, diffused light as he and his bride entered the room. On the table was a large bottle of champagne in a fancy container of ice. His bride knew of his alcoholic background and wondered about the wisdom of a champagne celebration, but she said nothing. As the night of romance glided along, the champagne bottle remained untouched in a sea of melting ice.

Dawn broke and his wife was singing in the bathtub. With the bottle in one hand, he knocked softly on the bathroom door. Then he popped the cork and champagne flowed down over her head and shoulders. With a twinkle in his eye and a sparkle in his voice, he said, "I christen you as my wife and pray that you will have a happy voyage through life with me." They laughed together.

That was beautiful imagination at work with a calculated element of surprise. Imagination is a tool which often lies unused in married life. Business as usual is the theme of day after day.

I believe God can whisper words to the listening ear of my soul through my imagination, and I believe he wants me to use this resource to bring spark and stimulation into my marriage.

The playboy philosophy encourages the world of fantasy. It promotes conjuring up passionate escapades with make-believe beauties. But Christians need not leave the fantasy world to playboys. You can let the playground of your mind be filled with visions of your mate and ways of expressing, "I think about you and I love you."

Love is full of fantasies.

I will help you grow

A tall, stately elm stood like a sentinel on duty. The trunk, three feet in diameter, held a crown of green foliage shaped like an enormous puff-ball. Ten feet from the base of this domineering elm was a sturdy oak fighting for its life. It was bent over as it reached out, attempting to grasp a beam of sunlight. But the elm had laid claim to the territory and held the younger oak in submission.

A beautiful fern graced our living room. The climate was conducive to rapid growth, but the roots had nowhere to go. As they searched for more soil from which to suck nourishment for the ever-expanding greenery, the walls of the small pot became an impregnable barrier. The fern was root-bound and its health began to wane. If it could not grow, death was the only alternative.

Plants need room to grow. So do people. Oliver Wendell Holmes said, "Most people die with their music still in them." In marriage it is easy for one to crowd out the potential of the other.

A marriage is composed of two unique creations of God. Both have received gifts that need nourishment in order to bloom. Wise partners hang on to each other with open hands so that neither suffocates in submission.

I must not only allow my wife to develop her interests and talents, I must encourage it. She then inspires me to explore my abilities and gives me the freedom even to fail. We don't grow in separate backyards, but side by side. We don't dream independently of each other, for we are one, yet two.

The home is not a place where one plant looms large and the other is dwarfed. The happy home finds two plants blooming with family fragrance, each rejoicing in the uniqueness of the other. Home also has plenty of room for some little plants, called children, to sprout and grow.

Love is giving room to grow.

I will be
a team player

A famous home run hitter comes up to the plate with a man on first and no one out. A home run would put the team ahead. He stands at the plate and mightily swings the bat, as though it were a toothpick. The muscles in his arms ripple with sinewy strength. As the crowd roars for the long ball, he looks down the third baseline. The coach signals "bunt."

The gladiator leads the league in home runs, and he's no great shakes as a bunter. But the order is to bunt! The team comes first. He obeys and the ball trickles off his bat. The runner advances and the next batter knocks him home.

In baseball we call that a "sacrifice," for the batter sacrifices his own interests to advance the cause of the team. The word "sacrifice" has a long history, and a proud one. You will find it in every situation of critical need. And the person who is willing to bunt when necessary is the person who plays well on any team.

Frank Sinatra used to sing a popular song, "I Did It My Way." People like that. We all

21

have a bit of peacock pride in us. It's easy to think that my way is always the right way. Thus every crossroad in marriage becomes a battleground where I stealthily plan and prepare to assure victory for my point of view. We have become indoctrinated with the belief that winning is everything. Thus we are tempted to keep score in everything we do. In personal relationships, the result of keeping score is devastating.

A marriage is a team endeavor. We often find it necessary to bunt in order to advance the needs of the other. What matters is not whether the husband wins or the wife makes more points. When the good of the team is the foremost pursuit, both husband and wife are winners.

Sometimes in the race of togetherness I must decrease the pace so my partner catches up with me. Sometimes she must slow up and hand the baton to me. We want to cross the finish line in family style.

Love is willing to come in second.

7

I will refuel romance

I came to the airport to await the arrival of
the beautiful brunette to whom I had decided
to pop the question. It was a frigid day, and
the chill winds evidently influenced my heart.
As she came down the flight stairs and floated
across the floor to where I was waiting, I ex-
tended my hand to her. The effect was disastrous.
After four months of not seeing me, she expected
a more exuberant welcome. I nearly blew the
courtship!

A respectable New Englander, proposing marriage over a century ago, had a firm hold on himself. He wrote: "I hope I have no foolishness
called romance; I am too well balanced for that
sort of nonsense. But we might look forward to
leading respectable and useful lives and enjoy
the respect of our neighbors." Few women
would nod in the affirmative to such a stagnant
statement.

You could measure your life by the number
of breaths you take. But maybe a better measure
would be the number of breathless moments

when you are caught up in wonder and ecstasy.

A woman anointed Jesus with a whole flask of precious perfume made from a plant that grew 3800 miles east of Jerusalem on the Himalayan Mountains. It perhaps cost her many months' wages. The disciples were indignant at the extravagance. Perhaps they said, "Go easy on that stuff, sister. It costs good money." There is no rational defense for her reckless, uncalculating act, but she was demonstrating deep devotion. Caught up in the moment, she completely forgot herself.

How did Jesus react to such surging spontaneity? His heart leaped. "Truly, I say to you, wherever this gospel is preached in the whole world, what she has done will be told in memory of her" (Matt. 26:13).

> Take all away from me
> But leave me ecstasy,
> And I am richer then
> Than all my fellow men.

In marriage, we must cherish the ability to let loose in reckless displays of affection and admiration. When it stealthily slips out of life, it takes so much with it.

Love is a moment of self-forgetfulness.

8

I will give you freedom

I drove into the driveway with a brand-new car. With bucket seats, padded dash, and luxury interior, it was a beauty, and I was intensely proud of acquiring it. When my children jumped in for a ride, I told them in no uncertain terms: Keep your feet on the floor, don't mess with the instrument panel, don't drop your gum, don't eat sticky candy. This new car was to be kept as clean as a surgical room in a hospital.

I didn't relish the idea of giving a bunch of rowdy boys from the church a ride. I was careful not to park too close to another car, afraid of a scratch on my car's polished finish. Something strange was happening to me in relationship to this machine on four wheels. It was beginning to possess me just as surely as I possessed it. We were getting locked together in a paralysis.

Better judgment began to prevail. The new car was to use as well as look at. While the children stuffed their mouths with popcorn, they were enjoying themselves. A scratch or dent wouldn't destroy the auto. Sitting loose in the saddle made driving a pleasant experience.

Sometimes in marriage we possessively guard our mates, making ourselves nervous and wary. We jealously hold on when they mingle with others, as though we might somehow lose their love. Obsessed with their good looks, we fear watching them grow old and wrinkled. We panic if disease threatens their life-style. We are devastated by the thought of our mate dying.

But wait a minute! What is marriage anyway? It is not possessing another person. It is a partnership where each can enjoy the other and have the privilege of sharing life and love. But God alone owns. All life belongs to him. God is so good that he entrusts us with the care and companionship of another of his children.

I cannot establish a proprietorship over my mate. She is not an appendage which I manipulate. She belongs to the Master of Life, and I must not suffocate her with possessiveness.

Love is not domineering.

9

I will let you be you

Procrustes was a devilish tyrant in Grecian mythology who had a bedstead to which he would tie any unfortunate traveler who happened to fall into his hands. If his captive was so tall that his legs stretched over the edge of the bed, Procrustes would promptly cut off his legs to fit. If the captive was shorter than the bed, Procrustes would torturously stretch him to fit the bed's dimensions. The victims of this cruel treatment were many.

In all mythical stories the tyrant sooner or later meets his master, and Procrustes was no exception. A young warrior by the name of Theseus overpowered the monster and slew him. However, Theseus neglected a very important matter when he disposed of Procrustes. He forgot to destroy the iron bed, which had a peculiar faculty of multiplying its own kind. So today the world abounds with little iron beds, whose owners try to fit others to the beds' dimensions, cutting here and adding there.

Descendants of Procrustes' bed seem to appear

in many master bedrooms. We pledge not to scissor up our mate when we say "for better, for worse," but soon we're sizing each other up for tailoring alterations. My wife is late and makes me wait. I tend not to talk when we go for a walk. She drives too fast. I don't look where I'm going. The list goes on and on.

After I once preached a sermon on molding a marriage, a young woman asked me for a copy. She said her husband could not be there that day and he needed to hear it. What she really meant was, "He needs to shape up and I want to clobber him with that sermon."

To be sure, both my wife and I need to change for the better. Marriage is always open to improvement. But frontal attacks seldom prompt improvement. No one ever slew the ancient dinosaurs. They merely passed into extinction when the climate changed.

I can't change my wife by verbal bullets. I will only make her cringe. She cannot harass me into being a harmonious husband. However, we can both love and support the best in each other so the climate of warmth and concern causes many of the little irritations to shrivel and die, or at least to lose their significance. Paul exhorts us, "Do not be overcome by evil, but overcome evil with good" (Rom. 12:21).

Love is acceptance.

10

I will look for the best

There is a story of a beggar who was sitting across the street from an artist's studio. The artist spied him and thought he would make an interesting portrait study, so from a distance he painted the dejected man. When he was finished he called the beggar over to look at it. "Who is it?" the beggar questioned.

Then he began to see a slight resemblance to himself. Hesitantly he asked, "Is it I?" The artist replied, "That is the man I see in you." The beggar said, "If that is the man you see in me, that is the man I'll be."

What do you see in your mate? If you spoon dignity out of the cup of your companion, you'll have left a dried-up shell. Whether you use words or reflected silence, your mate gets the message. Words like "stupid," "lazy," and "clumsy" are written in indelible ink, and the sketch is not pleasant. Your mate will live out the portrait you have painted.

If you lovingly paint the portrait, your mate's cup overflows with confidence. I have been blessed with a wife who sees much good in me. She doesn't gloss over my weaknesses, but she concentrates on my strengths. I'm no doubt a better man for her praise. If that is the man she sees in me, that is the man I'll be.

A tall girl in one of the congregations I served was very shy. She always walked slump-shouldered, and her smile was always at half-mast, as though she were in mourning. I made it a point to always compliment her, and a transformation began to take place. Soon she began to look beautiful.

Someone has wisely said, "The worst way to improve the world is to condemn it." This is also true of marriage companions. When Jesus stood before a sinful woman, he said, "Neither do I condemn you; go, and do not sin again." Jesus did not overlook her sin, but neither did he overlook her possibilities. He knew her shameful past, but he concentrated on her potential future. One person said of Jesus, "In the company of sinners, he dreamed of saints."

Love is seeing what could be.

11

I will laugh with you, not at you

In rabbinic story a student of the Torah announced to his rabbi that he was ready for ordination. The old teacher asked him what his credentials were. The young man replied, "I have disciplined my body so I can sleep on the ground. I eat the grass of the field and allow myself to be whipped three times a day."

"See yonder white ass?" asked the rabbi. "Be mindful that it too sleeps on the ground, eats grass, and is usually whipped more than three times a day. At present you may qualify to be an ass, but certainly not a rabbi."

I love humorous stories, but I am aware that jokes can jeopardize and puns may punish. Often our humor is at someone else's expense—it makes them look like an ass. It is reported that Lady Astor said to Churchill, "Winston, if I were your wife, I'd put poison in your coffee." Churchill responded, "If I were your husband, Nancy, I'd drink it." That story is double-barreled.

I am not advocating the abdication of jolly jokers, but I must warn that jokes may reveal how we consciously or subconsciously feel about our mates. Our camouflaged attitudes subtly surface in storytelling.

The danger lies in this: The more frequently we express our feelings, the more real those feelings become. Our frequent "put-downs" lower our regard for our mate, even if we speak jokingly. And when the water level of regard reaches a dangerous low, there is a marriage drought.

So start the pump of praise. Even if you praise your mate to friends and your mate doesn't hear, your words have a positive effect—you strengthen your love by expressing it.

"Her children rise up and call her blessed; her husband also, and he praises her: 'Many women have done excellently, but you surpass them all' " (Prov. 31:28-29).

Love is building up the other.

12

I will practice the proper touch

It was a warm summer day as I wheeled into the driveway. When I opened the car door, our stately German shepherd wagged his tail, staring at me with coaxing eyes. He lifted his large front paw as if to shake hands. I knew what he wanted. He enjoyed being scratched on his big barrel chest and he was not bashful about admitting it.

I have had other dogs, and each seemed to have a favorite spot to be scratched. One liked it behind the ear. Another would roll over for a belly rub. It was easy to detect where they wanted the massage, and I was always glad to accommodate their wishes.

Then one day I began thinking about how I greet and touch my mate. Perhaps the dog was scoring far too high on the scale of my attention. I asked myself: Do I greet the dog pleasantly, no matter how tired I am? What about my wife? Do I touch the dog where it most likes to be petted? What about my wife? Have I ever taken the time to discover where my wife enjoys being touched, or do I just touch her in ways that give me the most pleasure?

Today we talk a lot about verbal "strokes," but physical strokes are still very much in style. A bumper sticker with risque innuendos says: "If it feels good—do it." In the sacredness of marital union, partners can tell each other what feels good.

Some strokes are soothing, some exciting, some arousing. We ought to unashamedly reveal what sets off rockets of ecstasy and what soothes us into sleep. Then we should practice pleasing our partners.

It is right for a wife and husband to experiment in giving pleasurable feelings to each other. The apostle Paul puts it this way: "The husband should give to his wife her conjugal rights, and likewise the wife to her husband. For the wife does not rule over her own body, but the husband does; likewise the husband does not rule over his own body, but the wife does" (1 Cor. 7:3-4).

Let's try a little body language in saying, "I love you."

Love is pleasing each other.

13

I will keep myself for you

President Jimmy Carter admitted in a magazine interview that he had committed the sin of lust. While he had not physically broken the bonds of fidelity, he had fooled around in the playground of his mind. Some people were horrified at this confession. Others applauded his honesty, perhaps wishing that he had been a little naughtier. I admired him for revealing that sexual fidelity is a battleground, even for Christians.

Adultery is taboo with the God who created us male and female and who instituted marriage. History shows that adultery undermines the stability of a society built around home and family. Nevertheless, as with most sin, thought of an affair has a certain glamorous excitement.

A seminary friend of mine once said about a certain shapely sex queen, "Boy, she could eat crackers in my bed!" I knew that he was not a swinging guy. His statement simply revealed that her physical attributes had a way of getting to him. Lust may sweep into our hearts as easily as gossip slips out of our mouths. Both are wrong.

How do we keep lust from growing into actual unfaithfulness?

Coitus is not just a series of sexual mechanisms that give a momentary thrill. It involves the total person. That is why sexual union is for marriage. Unless it is part of a total relationship, it is incomplete.

Then I must think ahead. The pleasures of an affair have a strong pull, but they are short-lived. Only a loyal relationship to a spouse is good for the long haul. And life is not a series of sprints, but rather a distance race.

Also, I gave my word. My wife and I made a promise: "Keep thee only unto her (him) so long as you both shall live." That was the foundation on which we built. I cannot take my pledge lightly. So I agree with Robert Frost:

> The woods are lovely, dark and deep
> But I have promises to keep
> And miles to go before I sleep.

Love is commitment.

14

I will prime the pump

I remember well the old-fashioned water pump, especially the one in the middle of my hometown cemetery. As a boy I would spend lazy summer days filling a large bucket with water from the pump to pour down gopher holes. The rush of water down a hole would cause the gopher to come scrambling out and I would promptly snare him.

The pump always had to be primed. I had to pour water into the pump casing to get it started. Many things in life require certain actions before the mechanism will function. Human relationships also require priming.

In the Garden of Eden, when Adam and Eve violated God's decree, they panicked and hid in dense foliage. Their free and open relationship with their Creator was in jeopardy. But God initiated action to reestablish fellowship: "The Lord God called to the man, and said to him, 'Where are you?' " (Gen. 3:9).

Someone had to build a bridge so God and man could touch hands again. God did it with Adam.

And in the New Testament we read, "We love, because he first loved us" (1 John 4:19). God primed the pump. The Lord's love flowed into my being and caused my sluggish system to respond to the Savior's call.

Occasionally I have sat back like a spectator, wanting my wife to entertain me. I have passively expected her to start the business of seduction. Maybe that's not all bad, but it's far from being completely right. Men often look at women as instruments to "turn them on," and if they don't consistently do it, we call them cold cucumbers.

But we also have the job of priming the pump for the woman. The Scriptures talk about the responsibility of husbands loving their wives (Eph. 5:25). It seems that women were created with a built-in responder. When that is triggered by considerate, affectionate love from the husband, they turn into the delightful sexual creatures that God has enabled them to be.

A friend told me that when he discovered the secret of priming the pump and taking seriously his role of initiation, his wife responded with almost more love than he could handle. His cup was filled to overflowing.

Love is initiating action.

I will answer softly

There is an old fable of a careless hen in a farmer's barnyard. One day she accidentally stepped on the duck's foot. It didn't really hurt the duck, but he was touchy and he started to chase the hen. As he flapped after her, he hit the old goose with his wing. The goose thought this was deliberate provocation, so he took off after the duck, but in so doing, he brushed the cat, who was napping in the afternoon sun. The cat awoke with fire in her eyes and hissed, "I'll get you for that!" She leaped at the goose, only to land on the dog, who happened to get caught in the middle of the activity. The dog, who never did have a liking for the cat, seized on this opportunity for a declaration of war. He chased her into the barn. The cat zigged as the dog zagged, and the dog stumbled headlong into the cow, who kicked the milk pail, spilling the contents all over the floor. Such commotion there was! And it all started by a hen stepping on the foot of a duck.

Have you ever had a wasp buzz momentarily

around your head as you amble in the backyard in the summertime? If you don't bother it, chances are it will go away. But if you try to swat it, you arouse its indignation, and sting you it will.

Maturity in marriage is the art of learning to roll with the punches, and also knowing and respecting your spouse's vulnerable or sensitive areas. We all need to subdue and conquer over-sensitivity to slights. The wise author of Proverbs put it well: "A soft answer turns away wrath, but a harsh word stirs up anger."

Jesus shows us the way. He was accused falsely. He was taunted, mocked, and reviled. He was spat upon. But there were no shouts of condemnation from his lips. There was no reviling in return. There was only a prayer uttered for the forgiveness of the taunters.

Respect the "soft spots" of your mate—fat, or tardiness, or the relatives. If you're concerned about keeping the peace, you'll avoid contentious comments. No need to wave the red flag in front of the bull.

Someone asked an elderly woman who was well liked what her secret was in keeping so many friends. "Well," she said, "there's just one daily rule I follow. I'm always mighty careful to stop and taste my words before I let them pass my teeth."

Love is slow to anger.

16

I will label my actions

In the winter of the year, assorted jars of jelly are stacked on our basement shelf. They are not only the extra fruit of an abundant season, but also the fruit of my wife's labor. These jellies enhance a slice of toast on a cold winter morning. The jars aren't labeled and we guess the contents by color. Occasionally we are surprised by the type of jelly in a particular jar.

Actions, like jars of jelly, sometimes need labels to avoid confusion. I usually eat out at noon, but on this particular day I think it would be pleasant to eat with my wife. Suppose she is busy cleaning house and washing clothes. If I come bombing through the doorway and announce I'm home for lunch, chances are she won't seem overjoyed. Not planning to fix a noontime meal, she will probably think my arrival demonstrates lack of concern for her busy schedule, though I intended to show her that I enjoy her company.

Now the key to such a situation is that I quickly label my reason for coming home. If I put my arm around her and tell her I love her and want to spend the noon hour with her, she'll view my presence in a different light. And the sooner I speak, the better. We read the label on jars before tasting the contents. The reverse order is meaningless.

In the sacraments, God comes home to us. They dramatize his love. Yet when we celebrate the sacraments we preface them with words.

Actions by themselves can be misunderstood. Hosea says, "Take with you words and return to the Lord" (Hos. 14:2).

Don't forget to label your jars of jelly!

Love is speaking clearly.

17

I will
care for others

Traveling in the western mountains of the United States, I have often observed signs that say: "Beware—falling rocks." They alert travelers to impending danger.

The marriage road also has dangers of which travelers should beware. One is the attraction of pulling off the side of the road to enjoy the view. Some couples become so engrossed in their private lives that they "let the rest of the world go by." Wrapped up in their own concerns, they retire from any service to other people. They sink so much time, money, and effort into their home that they imprison their spirits therein.

Sometimes "things" are the problem—they climb into the saddle and ride us. Gadgets for good living become the goal, and payments become a permanent fixture. We intend to reach out to those in need, but we procrastinate, thinking that someday it will be different. In the meantime we are gaining the whole world of appliances and losing our own lives.

Antoine de Saint Exupery once said, "Life has

taught us that love does not consist of gazing at each other, but in looking outward together in the same direction." That is a dimension of love we cannot afford to miss. Windows of service not only permit us to look out at the world, they also permit the light of real life to shine in and energize the marital home.

Suppose you keep your backyard clean and tidy, but your neighbor's garbage cans are loaded to overflowing. When you have a picnic in your clean and tidy backyard, the flies breeding in your neighbor's garbage swarm down on your food. The way your neighbor lives affects you greatly.

No man lives or dies just unto himself. Each is responsible for all, and all are responsible for each. Humanity must be our business.

So the home becomes an outpost of love, mercy, and concern for others. It was never intended to be an isolated fortress to ward off the presence of other people. It is to be an extension of the Father's caring for the whole family of human beings. This larger family awareness will also intensify a couple's love for each other. The family that doesn't reach out will shrivel and die. Unconcern for others is a marriage crippler.

Love is reaching out.

18

I will love you with my mind

As we drove along on our honeymoon trip to Canada, we were reminiscing on our courtship days and our first feelings of love. I said, "You know, Fran, we *choose* to love." That sounded academic and calculating to her, and she responded rather coldly. She wanted to know if I had proposed to her because of the computer of my mind or the beat of my heart.

Feelings of love are necessary and basic, but I must also love with my mind. Jesus said, "You shall love the Lord your God with all your mind." A heart of gold and a head full of feathers will not create a happy marriage. The mind must be set on the course of love.

At seminary I had a friend from India, a handsome and brilliant lad. We tried to line him up with dates, but he always graciously declined. His father and elder brother had chosen a mate for him to marry when he returned to India. Amazed, I asked how he was sure they could pick out the right "beauty" for him. He simply stated that he trusted their judgment and that he would choose to love the woman they picked.

In his society, choice of mate preceded emotional involvement. That is not all bad. Love can grow out of deliberate, persistent goodwill. If the mind follows the path of love, the heart will take that course also.

The marriage based solely on feelings has a weak foundation. Feelings come and feelings go and feelings are deceiving. Some days we don't feel very loving. Maybe we don't even feel married. But the fact of determined love rides calmly through the storm and soon fact and feeling come together again.

When I married, I didn't promise to always feel on cloud nine about the ways of my wife. Such feelings could not be produced. Instead of promising what I would feel, I promised what I could choose to do: "To have and to hold from this day forward, for better or worse, for richer or poorer, in sickness and in health, till death do us part."

Love is a state of mind.

19

I will love our relatives

When Jesus knocks at the door of your human heart and you open it to let him in, he never enters alone. He always brings along his family, the communion of saints. Christianity has never been merely a cozy, private relationship between the believer and his Lord.

Marriage, too, is more than a cozy couple. Those folks we call in-laws are thrown in as a bonus in the marital contract. We don't vow to honor them and keep them in sickness and in health, but if we don't, we get into trouble. Still, responsibility for in-laws is not all bad. Such responsibilities characterize our Christian faith. We love others because he first loved us.

A married couple sat under a large oak tree, sipping ice tea and chatting with an out-of-town friend. They talked about their son, Mike, who was away for a stint in the army. Then the friend began to stare at the old dog sprawled out on the soft grass by the hammock. "Isn't it a nuisance to keep a dog here in town?" he asked.

"Yes, but old Boots belongs to Mike," they

explained. "They used to be inseparable buddies. Now that Mike's in the service, we're looking after his dog. And we love old Boots, too, for Mike's sake."

There it is—for Mike's sake. We love in-laws —even those who are a nuisance—for our mate's sake.

In the Book of Ruth we find a statement that is often sung at weddings: "Your people shall be my people." And that is the way it ought to be. I call my wife's mother "grandma." She is part of the family. I am blessed with a second mother.

Relatives should have the privilege of feeling that they belong. As you love them, you show love to your partner.

Love embraces others.

20

I will look for newness

Couples easily fall into the trap of boredom. In the songwriter's words, "Life sure gets tedious, don't it?" Two people tend to develop a treadmill existence—moving but not going anyplace. Life gets to be an endless addition of one day upon another, and sameness ties them all together.

> To-morrow, and to-morrow, and to-morrow
> Creeps in this petty pace from day to day
>
> . . . .
> It is a tale
> Told by an idiot, full of sound and fury,
> Signifying nothing.
>
> Shakespeare, *Macbeth* (V, v)

Husband and wife may slip into passivity which paralyzes their potential and zest for living. No spring rains fall on boredom, and marriage becomes as dull as dust in which nothing germinates. Between the happy home and divorce court come several stages, and perhaps the most evident is stagnation. A marriage that is merely holding its own may be in trouble.

Newness is as important to God's children as it is to his world of nature. Fruit always seems to grow on the new wood, the new shoots. In scripture God says, "Behold, I am doing a new thing" (Isa. 43:19). We have a creative God.

I must ask myself the question, "When am I dull?" I guess it is when I am totally predictable. If I do the same things in the same way day after day, life lacks luster.

My family has a music box that always plays the same tune. It has been playing that tune for 15 years. It can't help it—that's how it was constructed. But God doesn't program a person that way. A wide variety of music can burst forth from your soul.

Oldness in marriage is playing defensively. Newness is majoring in offense. We must risk the new. When I get the notion that I am contributing to a dull marriage, I must replace apathy with enthusiasm. I will no longer sit in the easy chair and watch my marriage go by, but I will arise and make things happen.

Turn your imagination loose and put a new idea into action. Dullness exits when discovery enters. Discover a new hobby, a new recipe, a new attitude, a new way of telling your mate, "I love you."

Love is risking change.

21

I will hear your viewpoint

One door and only one,
    And yet its sides are two.
I'm on the inside.
    On which side are you?

Once two knights on horseback were coming down a path from opposite directions, and they saw a shield tied to a branch of a tree. The first knight asked, "Who owns this white shield?" The second knight replied, "What do you mean, white shield—it is black as midnight." The first knight responded indignantly: "What do you think I am, blind or a fool? That shield is white." They drew their swords.

A third knight happened along and heard the commotion. He looked the situation over, then suggested that the two knights change places on the path. They soon discovered that one side of the shield was white and the other side was black. They were arguing because they hadn't taken the time to look at the issue from both sides. Sheepishly they saluted each other and went on their way.

Scripture says that in marriage two become one flesh. We swing together on the hinges of love and trust. But there are two sides to one marriage. Husband and wife are two unique persons with ideas and values that have grown out of their individual experiences and training.

Marital discord often arises when we do not have the patience or the wisdom to look at both sides of an issue. If we do pause to ponder our judgments, we become far less critical and the road is cleared for understanding.

Idea and person are wrapped up together like stripes on a candy cane. If you strip away a person's views, you are peeling his or her real being. That means if you do not take the time to listen or if you ignore your mate's opinions, you insult both the intelligence and personhood of your partner.

Love takes seriously the feelings and viewpoints of the other. It takes two to tango, and in marriage it takes two to decide.

Love is looking at both sides.

22

I will pause to wonder

The psalmist stood in awe, contemplating God's wondrous creation. "When I look at thy heavens, the work of thy fingers, the moon and the stars which thou has established; what is man that thou art mindful of him?" (Ps. 8:3-4). In a world surfeited with facts and scientific discovery, we have lost much of our sense of wonder, and we are poorer for the loss.

Elizabeth Barrett Browning was aware of the mysterious in nature.

Earth's crammed with heaven,
And every common bush afire with God;
But only he who sees takes off his shoes—
The rest sit round it and pluck blackberries.

Marriage brings together two miracles with the possibility of creating a third. Have you paused to wonder at these miracles?

Our sexual feelings are programmed chemical reactions set in motion by stimuli. Endocrine glands dump hormones into the bloodstream and they are circulated to their point of use. Thus sexual arousal is the result of the beautiful functioning of the laboratory of the body. We are wonderfully made.

Each of a girl baby's two ovaries contains up to 200,000 egg cells; about 400 ova eventually mature. After the female matures, the ovaries alternate in the monthly release of one ovum, which is smaller than a pinpoint.

God creates in abundance. A teaspoon of semen contains up to half a billion sperm. Each sperm is capable of uniting with an egg to create a new human being.

I don't advocate that, in a passionate embrace, husband and wife consider the mechanics of the possible miracle. But it is wise to pause and praise God occasionally for the enormous possibilities he placed within our human frames. Then we will hold lovemaking in reverence and awe. The mysterious is beautiful, and we should never be strangers to it.

Love is full of wonder.

23

I will keep singing

I have watched buzzards circling overhead looking for carrion. When they spot foul, decayed flesh, they plummet down to feed on it. I have also watched honeybees in search of sweet nectar, and they show discriminating taste as they fly among the colored vegetation of the garden. Both buzzard and bee find what they look for.

If we keep on the lookout for faults in our mate, we'll no doubt find them. But good qualities are also present, and we can choose to look for those.

A Swedish proverb says, "Those who wish to sing can always find a song." Frequently in marriage we are more prone to scold than sing. I find it easy to be like the crow who sits on a perch, criticizing and condemning what he observes. I find it more difficult to be like a cardinal, whose song lifts the spirit of all who hear. Maybe God gave the crow a coat of black because of its somber nature, and the cardinal got a royal red because it radiates joy.

Would that God would color me red. He wants to, but sometimes I'm unwilling to yield to his paintbrush. There is a legend that one day on a Far Eastern street, people were gathered around the body of a dog. In the East the dog is not a domestic pet, but a despised scavanger of the street. The bystanders thought the dead dog was repulsive. "How revolting," said one. "Loathsome," said another. Then Jesus came by and said, "But see how white its teeth are."

There is another old story of two grasshoppers who fell into a bowl of cream. One of them complained and groaned about his plight, and he sank to the bottom and drowned. The other kept singing and cheerfully kicked his feet. In time the cream turned to butter and he hopped away to freedom.

Marriages are doomed to drown if we constantly complain about each other. Our salvation is to have the mind of Jesus, who will put a song in our spirit. Then we will look for the silver lining, even in the darkest of clouds. We will realize that our mate is a prize, and thank God for his gift.

Love is seeking goodness.

24

I will strive for the best

We are impressed by quantity, whether it be of dollars, acres, jewels, or years of life. "The more, the merrier," becomes our motto—along with "The bigger, the better," for we also value size. Size determines how we rate a man's muscles or a woman's bosom. And we think a big diamond demonstrates how much a man loves his wife.

Size rules the roost, but its day is short-lived. The big diamond is little consolation in a marital crisis. The advent of old age brings sagging bosoms to women and muscular flab to men. Measurements have diminishing returns as the years go by. But quality abides. Whether in clothing or cars or marriage, only quality lasts.

Abundant living does not depend on the quantity of our activities, but their quality. We don't have to read everything, but we should choose what we read with care. Happiness depends, not on having everything, but on appreciating the quality of what we have.

Everyone must learn sooner or later the sage

advice: "Having one woman completely, he has all women, but seeking all women, he has none." If our goal in life is accumulating quantities, chances are we'll end up with nothing worth having.

It isn't the number of hours a couple sits in easy chairs watching TV that makes for togetherness. Physical proximity does not add up to marital bliss. What counts is how moments together are used. A few minutes of gut-level sharing is far better than hours of small talk.

Dr. Alvin Rogness said, "The tragedy is not that men die, but that they have never lived." The tragedy in marriage is that some couples spend decades together without really getting to know each other. They never create together anything worthy of eternity.

So remember, quality counts more than quantity. You don't know whether your marital trip will be short or long, but pack your mutual bag with quality living.

Love is seeking quality.

25

I will give it my all

Dieting has become common in our country. Whether to capture the look of eternal youth or to flee the dangers of heart disease, everyone is trying to lose weight.

Those who aren't successful like to rationalize. Some stand in front of a mirror, pull in their stomachs, hold their breath, and decide things aren't so bad after all. Some blame the split in their pants, not on bulging flesh, but on manufacturers who don't make things the way they used to. Others claim that according to the weight charts, they're just four inches too short.

A lot of dieting is just full of sound and fury, signifying nothing. Most people go at it in spurts, and then they sputter. They'd prefer a pill that would handle their excess baggage so they could go happily on—business as usual. But sincere weight watchers do their homework at the dinner table and also their roadwork on the exercise course faithfully day by day.

Marriage takes the same kind of determination. High blood pressure in marriage is caused by fat clogging the veins of communication. Overindulgence in selfishness, jealousy, and deceit adds up to a kind of obesity that drags down the health of a home.

No crash diet will quickly dispose of these dangers in marriage. Either we live sloppily with excess weight, inviting marital cardiac arrest, or we accept the necessity of discipline and struggle as the way to healthy living. If we're willing to strive for the worthy goal of a loving home, we must scrutinize those bulges on the marital body, then commence to work them off together by the exercise of prayer and running dialog.

George Grey Barnard, a noted sculptor, said, "Only through constant struggle do we grow or attain victory. The struggle in life is the important thing." No good thing comes without a struggle, whether it be health or a happy home.

Love is working at it.

26

I will be gentle

I was rolling down the freeway, enjoying the scenery and listening to soothing music on the radio. Suddenly I heard an explosion. I realized a tire had blown out. The smooth ride became bumpy before I could bring the car to a stop.

As I was changing the tire, I wondered what it would be like to drive at high speeds with all four tires flat. I guess only the pioneers in their covered wagons could describe that.

What a difference air makes in a tire! It enables a car to glide over the road. What is it that enables a marriage to glide along the road of life? The answer could be summed up in the word "kindness." Kindness is the air in matrimonial tires that gives couples a jolt-free ride. "Love is . . . kind" (1 Cor. 13:4).

Oliver Wendell Holmes said, "Good breeding is surface Christianity," but courtesy seems to be a vanishing species. Certain people never swear, but they make everyone else want to. That happens when the ingredient of kindness is not liberally sprinkled across our relationships.

William Barclay has pointed out that in Greek the word for grace and the word for charm are the same. So a Christian living by grace ought to have charm. Voltaire once said, "We cannot always oblige, but we can speak obligingly." So we can, and we must.

The marital ride would be more enjoyable if each partner practiced the art of being kind. Take out the book of etiquette and remember that manners belong in marriage. Most marital graves are not excavated overnight, but rather, by a series of little digs. Coarse belching words and actions take their daily toll. But kind words demonstrate loving concern, and they keep a home happy.

Be kind. Try it tonight.

Love is the squeeze of gentleness.

27

I will face the future

A young married couple settled down in a rented house in a new development area. The house made a cozy nest, but the lawn outside the house was almost naked. A few green tufts were the only vegetation in evidence. Sally told Bill that a few trees and shrubs would really enhance the property, but Bill wouldn't consider it. "We're paying good money for renting this place," he argued, "and we're not going to throw money away building up its value for the owner." That settled that. Nothing was planted.

Several years slipped by, with Sally and Bill still occupying the house. One day the owner came by and proposed that Sally and Bill purchase the place. His price seemed reasonable and within the reach of their finances. They completed the transaction shortly thereafter.

The following spring Bill went to a local nursery and bought several shade trees and ornamental shrubs to dress up their newly acquired property. Sally, observing her industrious husband as he proudly planted the nursery stock, couldn't resist commenting, "Bill, if you'd planted those trees the first year we moved in we'd be enjoying a little shade already." Bill nodded. But at that time he hadn't thought they'd still be living there, much less owning the property.

Most of us are prone to spot-thinking. Short-range goals are easier to cope with. Marriages can easily revolve around daily activities. We fail to plant for a fall harvest, then get upset because the foliage of family life seems so sparse.

We state at our wedding, "until death do us part." Death is usually many miles of living down the road. We must keep this in mind if we are to have a proper perspective on the present. Thus, the early days of marriage may not always be blissful, but if we keep planting prayer, patience, and principles, someday we will reap the fruit.

I've heard people say, "Well, things will be different when my ship comes in." That is often wishful thinking. Unless you send a ship out to sea, none will come in. I never go to the mailbox expecting to receive dividends from General Motors, for I have never purchased any stock.

Scripture tells us, "Do not be deceived; God is not mocked, for whatever a man sows, that he will also reap" (Gal. 6:7). So keep thinking about relaxing in the shade tomorrow, and patiently plant trees today.

Love looks ahead.

28

I will keep love hot

One person told me that marriage is like a hot teakettle placed on a cold stove—it soon cools off. Unless we take precautions, that can happen. Electrical current must constantly surge through the coils.

In Revelation, the church at Ephesus is commended for orthodoxy and endurance. "But I have this against you, that you have abandoned the love you had at first" (Rev. 2:4). Their love had cooled off. But love can be reheated and relationships can be rebuilt. "Remember then from what you have fallen, repent and do the works you did at first" (Rev. 2:4).

"Remember" — that is the first step. James Barrie said, "God has given us memories that we might have roses in December." When winter winds have cooled off the romance of marriage, the warm breezes of memory may bring back life to the frozen ground.

I remember my first meeting with the young woman I was to wed. As she descended the stairs to the living room of her country home, she looked like a fresh flower, and a beautiful fragrance announced her presence. I remember walking in a green meadow near a Minnesota lake as she slipped her hand into mine and squeezed it. I remember her kissing me as she was wheeled into the labor room, where she soon gave me our first son. Such memories can ignite love if it burns low.

"Repent"—that is the second step. Love is saying you're sorry. Confession is still good for the soul. Stones will not evaporate on a sunny day; neither will sins of indifference and hurt. Stones can only be cast away, and wrongs can only be confessed away.

Finally, I must "do the works" I did at first. And I remember what they were! I proudly told my friends about the young woman who had captured my heart. I drove out of my way to see her. I searched for time to be alone with her, and I always found it. I looked for ways to surprise her. I didn't need a birthday or holiday— every day in young love was special, and reason enough for celebration.

Love does not grow without cultivation. But with proper care it will be a perennial bloomer.

Love is as big as we make it.

29

I will give myself away

Husbands and wives have been exchanging gifts from time immemorial as a way of showing that they care. But gifts can also be used to manipulate.

Sometimes we give gifts to display our generosity. A husband is more likely to buy a corsage for his wife than a bouquet for the living room table. Why? Everyone will see the corsage and think what a fine, considerate husband he is. Jesus had stern words for those who tried to pull this stunt on God. Some of the most fun gifts are nonutilitarian and no-show. They may even be riotously inappropriate and ludicrous such as:

> On the first day of Christmas
> My true love gave to me
> A partridge in a pear tree.

Such gifts are surprises that say: "You're special."

Another adulterated gift is the one we wrap in a didactic attitude. Maybe a wife wants her husband to be more spiritual. She hears of a good book on the subject. She buys it, wraps it, and presents it to her husband as a loving gift. But an odor of foul play surrounds it. The gift is her attempt to change her husband's ways. There are strings attached. Her motives may be good, but her means are devious.

Gifts may also be used as bribes, to dominate others: Be a good boy or girl and you will be rewarded. If you give a big gift, you may want to make your mate feel indebted. He who pays the piper calls the tune.

O. Henry caught the real kernel of gift-giving in his lovely Christmas story. A husband and wife wanted to give each other the gift that each longed for. The husband wanted a chain for his watch and the wife wanted a comb for her beautiful long hair. But times were hard and money was scarce—they couldn't afford even these small gifts. So the husband secretly pawned his watch to buy the comb. At the same time, the wife cut her long hair and sold it so she could buy the chain for her husband's watch. Christmas Eve might have been a catastrophe! But no, their selfless giving bound them in a golden cord of love.

Let each small gift reflect God's great gift in Jesus Christ—there are no strings attached.

Love is giving selflessly.

30

I will try to understand

Spirits do not always soar. Sometimes even the noblest of spirits sinks into a despondent sea. Elijah, the Old Testament prophet, serves as an example. He stood in triumph on Mount Carmel as his God defeated the prophets of Baal. His courage and faith were dauntless. Yet a short time later, a lonely figure dragging his feet across the parched Arabian desert, he collapsed on the shifting sand and cried out: "It is enough; now, O Lord, take away my life; for I am no better than my fathers" (1 Kings 19:4).

How did Elijah get so low that he desired escape from life itself? After a 200-mile flight on foot with little food and water, he was physically depleted and depressed. In such a state, a person's statements should not be held against him.

Your mate, if physically or emotionally exhausted, may occasionally speak harshly. But remember that a mariner takes his bearings when the sun or stars are visible, not in the confusion of clouds. Cast off the caustic remarks your mate makes in a despondent mood, understanding that they would not have been made in the sunshine.

Another reason Elijah was discouraged was that he was thinking of how King Ahab and Queen Jezebel hated him. As he fled from their wrath, he became convinced that everyone had turned against him. After Elijah had eaten and regained his strength, God gently reminded him that 7000 in Israel had not bowed to Baal.

After some bout with life, when it seems the whole world is against him or her, your mate may feel that even you couldn't care less. At such times, don't chastise your partner for being silly. Rather, show that you love and believe in your spouse.

Love is understanding.

31

I will love you even if you fail

Our society tells us we have to win or be stamped as second-class citizens. As a result, some people are paralyzed by fear of failure. Too timid to try something new where the outcome might be in doubt, they function only in a circumscribed realm where there is not room for falling flat on the face.

Husbands and wives are sometimes inhibited by this failure complex. They feign happiness so their marriage won't appear a failure. The wife pretends to be fulfilled at home so no one will brand her an incomplete homemaker. The husband secretly wants to try another vocation, but rather than look like a quitter, he plods along. Both are "uptight" about sex, afraid of being a lousy lover or incapable of orgasmic ecstasies. They neither enjoy life nor suffer much, because they live in a twilight zone that knows no real victory or defeat.

One day I watched a wren building a home in a small birdhouse in our backyard. Attempting to get a rather large twig into the small hole, several times she dropped it to the ground. She would then fly down, pick it up, and try again. In the midst of her failures she occasionally paused for a few bursts of song. Never once did she hide her head under her wing, embarrassed by her unsuccessful attempts. Finally, she picked up the twig near the end and maneuvered it through the opening. Failure was neither fatal nor final for this little winged creature.

Jesus gave his disciples room for failure. He told them that when the gospel fell on deaf ears they must learn to shake off the dust from their feet and move on—a sacrament of failure that enabled them to lose and then try again, always at the risk of not standing in the winner's circle. Peter knew the healing balm of an understanding look from Jesus in the courtyard after his denial of the Lord.

Husbands and wives need to give each other the right to fail. Then they each can step to the plate and swing boldly, not fearing chastisement for striking out. There will be another day and another chance.

Love is resilient.

32

I will keep saying it

A young girl who was dying was hearing for the first time the story of God's love. "God loves you. God sent his son, Jesus, to die for you so all your sins are forgiven. He wants to take you home with him." Her eyes opened wide at the amazing story. She exclaimed, "Tell me again!"

During my college and seminary days, every time I left home after a brief visit, my father would say two things: "Jim, I love you, and I will be praying for you." I never tired of hearing that. I welcomed his words again and again.

Peter and Mary were standing by the jukebox at the old truck stop. Mary said, "Peter, play A-3—please!"

"Mary," he said, "you don't want to play that same old song again. You listen to it all the time!"

"Well, I happen to like it," retorted Mary. "When I get paid for mowing the lawn this weekend, I'm going to buy that record and play it over and over again."

Sometimes we crave new things and new expressions. Routine can be boring. Words become trite and archaic. But some expressions never grow old. They are always warm and exciting. They burrow into the heart of what really matters.

Whether spoken after a session of spark-making love or when husband and wife part for work at the dawn of day, the words "I love you" envelope the beloved with a never-tiring caress.

When a mate comes back from a conference meeting or a trip to grandma's place, the words "I missed you" are like gentle rain on thirsty soil.

When a person has been floored by disappointment, there is no balm quite like the words "I believe in you."

So say it again.

Love is a lovely word.

33

I will tell you when I'm upset

President Truman once said, "If you can't stand the heat, get out of the kitchen." Many people use this principle to govern their lives. If things get a bit sticky, they pack their bags and move on. They are always looking for an easier key in which to play the music of life.

Today many wives and husbands simply drop out when the marital road gets rough. But running away never solved a problem. When Joe Louis was in training for his fight with Billy Conn, a newspaper reporter told him that Conn was practicing his footwork and he hoped to keep away from Joe's lethal fists. Louis thought a minute, then smiled as he said, "He can run, but he can't hide."

There's no hiding place in the boxing ring. There's really no place to hide in life's ring, either. We can run, but we'll never get away. True boxing skill lies not in fancy footwork, but in slugging it out. The marriage ring is not a place for skirting personality conflicts and problems, but for verbally slugging it out.

Anger is bound to arise when two imperfect human beings live side by side. Scripture can attest to this. But we should heed the warning: "Do not let the sun go down on your anger" (Eph. 4:26). Don't flee from anger, don't panic and take a walk, for the problem will pursue you. Don't, in the words of Robert Burns, "nurse your wrath to keep it warm." Rather, listen to your partner. Anger has to be released. Let the venom spew forth.

After many boxing matches I've observed the two fighters throw their arms around each other and exchange words of congratulations. So may a husband and wife embrace after their anger has been released. Then, and only then, will healing take place.

Don't nurse your anger. Take it into the ring. *Love is not afraid of confrontation.*

34

I will use God's blueprint

There was once a rich man who wanted to do a good thing. He noticed the miserable condition of a poor carpenter, so he commissioned him to build a beautiful house. "I want this to be an ideal dwelling," he said. "Use only the best materials, employ the most skilled craftsmen, and spare no expense." The rich man said he would be going on a journey and he hoped the house would be finished when he returned.

The carpenter saw this as a great opportunity to make a few extra bucks. Therefore, he skimped on materials. He hired inferior workers at low wages and covered their mistakes with paint and veneer.

When the rich man returned, the carpenter showed him the house and said, "I have followed your instructions. Here is the finished product."

"Good," said the rich man. Then he handed the house keys to the carpenter and said, "They are yours. I had this house built for you. You and your family are to have it as my gift." The carpenter's smile sagged into a frown.

A married couple may wake up one day to find that their marital roof is leaking, the foundation of faith is sagging, the walls of integrity are leaning, and they wonder if the old home they built is worth saving. But it's all they've got. And repair jobs are costly.

God gives us the equipment to put together a marital mansion. He supplies us with the finest tools. But other things demand our attention and entice our desires, so we think we can sloppily slap it together. We forget that it is ours for a lifetime, and that it will take time and energy to build it properly.

You must start with a good blueprint. Check God's Word for that. Use faith for the foundation. The lumber should be the finest grade of love. Putty all the windows with prayer. Trim the house with trust. Furnish it with forgiveness.

Your home will be as fine as you want to make it. Start by doing all the little things in a great way.

Love is building for eternity.

35

I will make our house a home

A jokester said, "A marriage is like stepping into a bathtub; after you get used to it, it ain't so hot."

Many marriages are based merely on coexistence. Couples share what Thoreau called "lives of quiet desperation." When money bickering replaces lovemaking, when silence replaces concerned communication, when mates become islands rather than one flesh—that isn't a marriage, it's a cold war.

If your mate is tempted to fly the coop and roost somewhere else, ask yourself, "Is this place worth coming home to? Am *I* worth coming home to?"

If you're not sure, you'd better start refurbishing the nest with the down of kindness, gentleness, and self-giving love. Remember, the Prodigal Son went back home because his father's love and forgiveness were worth going back to.

One man I know spends most of his hours in a local bar, sipping away the day. His marriage is on the brink of disaster. Certainly he is wrong in attempting to plug the holes in his life with booze—it will never do the job. But after I heard a yelling contest between him and his wife, I could empathize a bit. He came home inebriated to cushion himself from her attacks.

After a day of combat with the world, neither man nor woman wants to come home to a war zone. Home should be like an oasis for the weary desert traveler. And it can be that way.

Love is worth coming home to.

36

I will be standing by

If you have a few years on your calendar of life, you will remember the days before there were long-play records or tapes. All radio programs were live. If technical difficulties arose, the program would have to be interrupted and the announcer would say, "Will you please stand by?" During the break there would be music—live music. The major networks hired orchestras to stand by for such emergencies. At a moment's notice they had to be ready to play. They were called standby orchestras.

I have a strong conviction that God wants us to be standby people. At airports I enjoy watching passengers' faces as they spot loved ones standing by, waiting for them. A short time ago after back surgery, when I was wheeled out of the postoperative room, my wife was standing there waiting. She needed to say nothing. Having her standing by was therapy for my soul.

You may not know how to take away the suffering of another, but you can stand by. You may not be able to solve someone else's problem, but you can stand by. You may not always have the words to express your feelings, but you can stand by.

In boxing matches, each contestant has a corner of the ring where his aides and coach minister to him. After he is battered and bruised, what if no one were waiting in his corner? Perhaps he would lose the courage to continue the fight.

Life is that way. The psalmist was in deep despair when he said, "No one cares for my soul." We all need someone in our corner. A man told me that while his wife was in the hospital his home became just a house, like any other house. But when she was there waiting for him, it was home, a beautiful place to be.

If you care, you will be standing by whenever your presence is needed.

Love is being there.

37

I will take inventory

A nine-year-old boy wanted to be a saint. He had read many stories of saints in the history of the church, and best of all he liked the story of Simeon Stylites, who had perched on top of a pole for many years. In monastic style, he lived on his pole like a statue. People came to see him, thinking that he was quite a holy man.

This nine-year-old boy thought he would re-enact the whole procedure, so he put a stool in the middle of the kitchen floor and announced to his mother, "I'm going to stay here for 40 years." It didn't take long for him to realize that he was getting in the way of the rest of the family. In fact, his mother told him he was a first-class nuisance. Soon she told him to move his stool and go somewhere else to play his games. As the lad picked up his stool and walked dejectedly into the living room, he said, "It's hard to be a saint when you're living at home."

No doubt about that. Saintly behavior is hard to maintain at home. It is tough to imitate the life of Jesus among those who know us inside out.

The little boy who wanted to be a saint had a worthy goal, but a poor method. He didn't take into consideration those with whom he was living. Do you sometimes allow seemingly worthy goals to disrupt your relationship with your mate?

We must be lifelong students of the art of living together. Paul exhorts the church at Corinth, "Examine yourselves, to see whether you are holding to your faith. Test yourselves. Do you not realize that Jesus Christ is in you?—unless indeed you fail to meet the test!" (2 Cor. 13:5). We must check often to be sure our conduct coincides with our creed.

I've developed a questionnaire for checking my marital I.Q.

1. Am I easy to live with?
2. Am I easily hurt or offended?
3. Do I manifest the spirit of forgiveness and understanding?
4. Will my mate see Jesus in me?
5. Am I in the way or helping my mate on the way?

If I score low, I need not despair. With God's grace, I can take the test again, and with his help I will score well.

Love is being easy to live with.

38

I will seal you with the cross

We knelt at the altar near the close of the wedding service. As the pastor pronounced the benediction, he made the sign of the cross with his right hand. The ceremony was over, but the mark of the cross lingered in our lives.

This symbol of a crucified Christ declares that God has cancelled the debt of our sin. He blots out our iniquity and the guilt of our errors. The forgiving love which the cross symbolizes is the only way I know to manage marital mistakes.

Jesus laid claim to us at Calvary. Receiving his claim, you and I no longer live unto ourselves, but unto him. His mark of ownership is upon us. Therefore, I look on my mate as a gift from God. She is loved by God and has eternal worth. "From now on, therefore, we regard no one from a human point of view" (2 Cor. 5:16).

Another symbol I like to keep in mind is the plus sign. Jesus came that we could have life and have it abundantly. He was not a negating person. He seemed never to subtract, always to add.

I find it easy to be a minus man. Carping criticism at home always cuts. It's minus stuff. If you cannot say anything kind, say nothing at all.

A plus person brings life to a marriage. Luther told us how to be plus people when he gave meaning to the Eighth Commandment: "Apologize for him, speak well of him, and put the most charitable construction on all he does."

Stand opposite your mate and seal each other with the sign of the cross.

Love is remembering Christ's claim.

39

I will pray for us

Nuclear energy has been sustaining life on the face of the earth from the beginning of time, for the sun runs its lighting and heating facilities from this power source. Our lives depend on it, but not until recently did we begin to understand it and utilize it. So it is with many people and prayer power.

Spiritual energy is an endowment. We cannot create it, but God gives us the privilege of plugging in and using it for his glory and for our own growth in grace. Yet many couples fail to take advantage of the power available to them through prayer.

It's easy to gripe, "My mate doesn't cooperate. I have to carry the whole load." It's easy to concentrate on the faults and foibles of the other. But through prayer God gives you a mirror that reflects the positive side of your mate.

You'll also find yourself reflected in the mirror. You'll find yourself asking, "Why did I say that? Did I purposely hurt her?" Persistent prayer will change your outlook, removing obstacles to love. Jesus said to pray even for enemies.

We've all seen the motto "Prayer changes things." That's true, but even better is the motto "Prayer changes me."

Try it! The next time your mate irritates you, bring it to God in prayer. Open yourself to God's grace for whole relationships.

Love is looking upward.

40

I will keep climbing

A boy won a prize for a drawing he made for the Sunday school exhibition. When someone congratulated him for his fine work, he said, "That isn't my best drawing."

"Why didn't you exhibit your best?" he was asked.

"Oh," he replied, "my best drawing isn't drawn yet." That boy was on the road to becoming a good artist.

Browning said, "Grow old along with me! The best is yet to be." Many will respond, "Hogwash!" Old age has its aches and pains, its sagging flesh and loss of vigor. But growing old together can bring mellowness, achievement, and tranquility. Your later years may be your best years.

In June 1940, Winston Churchill flew to Tours, France. Returning, he called a special session of the British war cabinet. He reported to them that France was on the verge of caving in and asking Hitler for his terms. Reviewing the dismal military and political outlook, Churchill summed it up by saying, "We are now facing Germany completely isolated." A silence fell across the group. Churchill then looked up and said, "I find it rather inspiring." The British statesman was 66 years old.

Each stage of life has its hurdles and its special rewards. God provides fruits for all seasons. Life can be like a spiraling crescendo moving upward and onward. The best way may be the tomorrows if you keep searching and striving.

And traveling two by two is the best way I know to climb the mountains of life. Each plateau is special, and when you and your mate stand together, each achievement is doubled in joy.

Love is growing old together.

Prayer for partners

Lord, we believe that you ordained marriage and
that you also sustain it. Help us to exercise faith.

> Faith that you answer prayer and heal
> wounded hearts.
>
> Faith that you forgive and restore.
>
> Faith that your hand of love will clasp
> our hands together.
>
> Faith that you build bridges of reconcilia-
> tion.
>
> Faith that all things will work for good to
> those who love you.

Help us to hold on to hope.

> Hope that enables us to endure times of
> trial and testing.
>
> Hope that fixes our gaze on possibilities
> rather than problems.
>
> Hope that focuses on the road ahead in-
> stead of detours already passed.
>
> Hope that instills trust, even in the midst
> of failure.
>
> Hope that harbors happiness.

Help us to lift up love.

> Love that doesn't falter or faint in the winds of adversity.
>
> Love that is determined to grow and bear fruit.
>
> Love that is slow to anger and quick to praise.
>
> Love that looks for ways of saying "I care for you."
>
> Love that remains steady during shaky days.

Lord, may your gifts of faith, hope, and love find plenty of living room in our hearts. Thank you that these three abide—and the greatest is love. Make our home an outpost for your kingdom and an oasis for wandering pilgrims. In the name of Jesus who blessed the marriage at Cana with a miracle. Amen.

The way of love

And I will show you a still more excellent way. If I speak in the tongues of men and angels, but have not love, I am a noisy gong or a clanging cymbal. And if I have prophetic powers, and understand all mysteries and all knowledge, and if I have all faith, so as to remove mountains, but have not love, I am nothing. If I give away all I have, and if I deliver my body to be burned, but have not love, I gain nothing. Love is patient and kind; love is not jealous or boastful; it is not arrogant or rude. Love does not insist on its own way; it is not irritable or resentful; it does not rejoice at wrong, but rejoices in the right. Love bears all things, believes all things, hopes all things, endures all things. Love never ends (1 Cor. 12:31—13:8).